HEAL

How To Deal With And Rise Above Sad Experiences

Pat Uche Nwulu

Copyright © 2020 by Pat Uche Nwulu

Cover design: PatUch Concepts

Published by: PatUch Concepts

Email: patuchconcepts@gmail.com

+234 706 898 7100

DEDICATION

In memory of my beloved father, Rev. Canon Samuel Bemenjo Nwulu (of blessed memory). I miss all the moments we spent together, Dad. Your memory lives on!

This piece is dedicated to my wonderful family—my mom and siblings. We have learned to bond and stay together, and have endured and healed through hard times and Daddy's demise together. I love you all

ACKNOWLEDGEMENT

Thanks to God Almighty, who has filled me with every wisdom and has provided me with the comfort of the Holy Spirit, to deal with and rise above hard times.

I have the best siblings ever, and every day I am grateful to God for the gift of my siblings. I love you all so much (Mrs. Gloria Idemoh, Victory, Gift, Gideon, and my babies, Owen and Jason)!

Thank you all so much for the support and unity. Thank you for being the most vital support system and special rescue squad. Thank you, Mom (Mrs. Dorothy Okwukwe Nwulu), for loving us dearly and being strong for us.

I especially thank my beloved personal assistant, Miss Gift, who makes it possible for me to meet tight deadlines. You are simply amazing, keep up the good work.

Dear Nwachukwu Chinedu Ogbonna, you are the most amazing person on earth. Thank you for being a true friend. Thank you for always praying for me.

Special thanks to Accelerated Capacity Enhancement (ACE Consult), the dedicated team of Nation Builders, for giving me a platform to put forth my skills and contribute my quota to nation-building and making our world a better place.

Thank you so much, Lead Coach Victor Akuro, you are indeed a selfless life coach and leader, and I appreciate your effort, availability, and mentorship.

Thank you so much, Mrs. Ugochi Ekezie-Ntui, for agreeing to write the foreword to this book. Thank you for being a source of inspiration to other ladies out there and to me.

Dearest Pastor Uche Etiaba, thank you so much for loving me the way you do and for giving me wings to soar again. I especially thank everyone in my life who has contributed in many ways. God bless you all.

CONTENTS

PREFACE

Well, let me begin by saying that, as a lady, I have experienced jealousy, anxiety, irritability, longing, desire, pride, boredom, shame, laziness, worry, embarrassment, and feeling overwhelmed.

There have also been times when I felt enthusiastic, calm, hopeful, vibrant, inspired, courageous, happy, and even a sense of love. I have encountered every one of these things in my own life, and regularly, with a decent portion of battle en route.

Slowly, be that as it may, through my own investigations, research, perceptions, and encounters, I have become increasingly mindful of the force that we need to pick up when we feel what we feel. Over time, I have recognized and created systems to help adequately make this life-advancing cycle easier; I can say that I have grown through the storms.

In search of this fulfillment, which is an escape from feeling hurt, some turn to drugs and other habits. Mine was withdrawal. I derived so much pleasure from spending time with myself that I shut everyone out. So if you're reading this and remember the times I gave you terrible cold feet, I am so sorry. I was dealing with myself.

It became extreme; I was wasting away. It is easier to deal with the side effects rather than the cause of the pain and suffering. This does not always work, as emotions are to be expressed and pain is to be felt, not denied. As much as these beliefs exist, we must actively deal with and heal from them in order to live more balanced and happy lives.

On several occasions, you go through life encounters that can have a lot of effects and results on a passionate or deeper level—catastrophe, the passing of a loved one, lack of fulfillment in your own life, a misfortune, a horrible educational encounter, life conditions, and a previous memory can cause you a lot of agonies, enthusiastic pain, and injury.

If you are unaware of the significance of emotional healing, the likelihood that you will disregard it or try to suppress it is very high. Emotional hurt and pain can make you feel hopeless, weak, miserable, and awkward; they also have a lot of power over how you feel about yourself and life, and they can lead to misery if not addressed.

To adapt to the agony felt by many, this book will attempt to discover help by showing you how you can grow through and completely heal from any negative situation.

I carried the baggage of emotional hurts for several years, bled on people who did not hurt me, lost valuable relationships, and suffered some setbacks because I did not heal from the pain and hurt.

Going through these experiences, I had a clearer understanding of the importance of emotional healing and wholeness, and I also learned that we cannot ignore our emotions, as they are part of our inner experiences. Understanding the importance of emotional healing and taking the necessary steps to ensure wholeness brings about a life of peace, happiness, security, and more mature living.

This book is about our daily experiences: how we get emotionally involved in family, social life, business relationships, and even family problems; how to deal with and rise above the odds of life. More so, it reflects my inner struggles and triumphs as a sojourner.

I have shared my personal encounters and other stories to encourage you in this book. You have to know that healing is possible, regardless of what has happened. At the end of each chapter, there are very important and personal action points that you should take seriously. will review them in the last chapter. Read this book with an open mind and expect absolute wholeness.

Pat Uche Nwulu

FOREWORD

The world most times and even nature itself, throws hard and tough stones that do not just hit and create physical or obvious wounds on our flesh but goes deep into wounding our souls. Like the physical wounds, if ignored, it causes more harm and brings more pains on the carrier.

This book is a suitable tool to help heal the hearts and souls of those who have been trapped and held bound by the pain and memories of their past traumas and experiences, ranging from physical and/or sexual abuses, hatred, sibling rivalries, loss of loved ones, body shaming, depression etc.

Pat in this book, used her personal experience and vulnerable testimonies and life experiences of various individuals to put down detailed and step-by-step help for those who have been hurt and betrayed, to find courage and strength to face their pain and fear.

She also introduces us to the widely opened arms of God's love and His desire for us to walk into His warm embrace to fetch from His well of love and acceptance and also find ourselves through His Holy Spirit and His Word of love, peace, acceptance and encouragement.

Being a Life Coach and a relationship counsellor, I've come to realize that a lot of crises in marriage and other forms of relationships, are a result of unhealed wounds and untreated souls and heart injuries.

Carrying the baggage of hurt, pain and unforgiveness into a relationship always has a ripple effect on the partner and this has contributed to the increased number of heartbreaks, separation, divorce and even suicide due to depression.

"Heal" is here to offer that help and guide you need to come out of your 'Past', embrace your 'Today' and live out your 'Tomorrow' (your dreams).

I watched Pat grow out of the pain of losing a loved one - her beloved Father. I watched her break free from the inferiority complex and accepted herself for who she is; this has led to a great impact on everyone around her and the world at large.

Wouldn't you rather learn from someone who has been through that state of pain you are going through, and broke forth with great and visible testimonies?

Wouldn't you rather release yourself to be held by the hand through a step by step process and guidance on how to be healed? Yes, Healing is possible! But the desire to be healed is key.

Are you or anyone you know struggling with the pain and hurt of the past; depression, inferiority complex, abuse, rejection, unforgiveness, self-pity, body-shaming, hatred, etc.? Do you desire to be healed? Read this book with an open mind.

Don't skip a step. Allow God through this book to flow through your heart and soul and bring healing, and restore you to the true person that you are. Let go of the struggles and follow every laid down guide in this book. This book will help you through the healing process.

Ugochi Ezekie-Ntui

Certified Relationship & Marriage Mentor
Founder, International Women Fellowship (IWF)

CHAPTER 1:

IS HEALING POSSIBLE?

The burden of unforgiveness or not letting go is heavier and more dangerous than the pain of the ugly experience

We had a ladies' conference two years ago and we talked about some of the things women have to deal with as daughters, teenagers, career women, wives, and mothers.

It was an interesting time, and during the plenary session; Kim, a lady in her mid-thirties who was married with two kids, pointed out that there was no need for us to talk about the possibility of healing.

I became curious and tried to find out why, and she said that a lot of things have become normal and there was no point in trying to change them because they would not change. She further shared some very personal stories that had formed the basis for her belief system. At the end of the three-hour session, she broke down in tears, and we further booked a counseling session for her.

Why did I start with this story? A lot of people have come to terms with the fact that some things seem normal but, in reality, they are not. It is not normal to go through physical abuse and molestation as a person, and it is also not normal that you have to accept that it is normal.

Well, you might say, just like Kim, that these are the things we carry around with us in our everyday lives; but that doesn't make it normal.

A lot of people die every day from the suppression of emotions and realities that they deny simply because they feel there is nothing that can be done about the situation. This book will open your mind to the reality of healing.

Soul Wounds

First, the Bible says, "I wish above all things that you prosper and be in health, even as your soul prospers." So, it is the will of God that we stay in health, body, soul, and spirit.

You may have a lot going on in your life right now—unmet expectations, family problems, money issues, and all that—but I want you to know that irrespective of the weight of the circumstance, healing is possible; you don't have to go around bleeding in places no one can see.

Healing is not something that comes naturally to people who have faith. We can become permanently scarred when we are subjected to hurt and pain.

In any case, this sort of scarring is not quite the same as a skin scar, and the smallest trigger or occasion can make us react with conduct that really builds up the passionate injury, making a pattern of interminable woundedness.

If we keep ignoring this aspect of our lives instead of addressing our emotional or soul wounds, the foe will keep having a fortress in this space. Soul wounds can be a part of us for so long that we acknowledge them and are really hesitant to be freed of them.

In 2016, I lived in a local compound where we lived as a family; there were only 3 families in the whole compound, so associating was not a big deal.

I watched my neighbor, John, go through the injury of nearly losing his 10-year-old daughter in an automobile accident years prior. He was driving with his girl in the front seat when they were struck head-on by another vehicle on the passenger's side of the vehicle.

The trauma of the event, particularly the realization that his daughter may have been genuinely harmed or slaughtered, has resulted in post-traumatic stress disorder and stress issues. Till date, when a vehicle is moving toward him from the traveler's side, he displays an antagonistic response.

I've come to understand that post-awful pressure, stress and emotional problems are a kind of a soul or emotional wound that we must heal from.

So are dismissal, relinquishment, and threats to separate a couple. Actual illnesses can be caused by an injured soul just as much as bothersome practices.

An injured soul gives a place for the foe, the demon, to inconvenience even the most dedicated Christian. There is a need to comprehend the domain of soul wounds so as to experience the healing and completeness Christ passed on to give us.

So, where do we start from when we begin to talk about healing? It could be healing of the mind and body. For the purpose of this book, we will dwell more on the healing of the soul, which comes from within.

Soul wounds are not like regular physical wounds, which are obvious to all; that is a major reason they should be given maximum attention. A person can be smiling while he or she is bleeding or broken on the inside.

Do You Desire to Be Healed?

After this there was a feast of the Jews, and Jesus went up to Jerusalem. Now there is in Jerusalem by the Sheep Gate, a pool, which is called in Hebrew,

Bethesda, and has five porches. In these lay a great multitude of sick people, lame, andd, lame, paralyzed, waiting for the moving of the water.

For an angel went down at a certain time into the pool and stirred up the water; then whoever stepped in first, after the stirring of the water, was made well of whatever disease he had.

Now a certain man was there who had an infirmity of thirty-eight years. When Jesus saw him lying there, and knew that he already had been in that condition a long time, He said to him, "Do you want to be made well?"

The sick man answered Him, "Sir, I have no man to put me into the pool when the water is stirred up; but while I am

coming, another steps down before me."
Jesus said to him, "Rise, take up your bed
and walk." And immediately the man
was made well, took up his bed, and
walked.

This is a story in John chapter five from verse one to verse eight. The man in the story had been bedridden for a very long time; he had become so used to his situation that he had forgotten what it felt like to be made whole.

He probably no longer had any pictures in his head. But something miraculous happened to him—the Lord, in His gracious and kind nature, approached him with a swift offer that he had been waiting on for the past thirty-eight years of his life.

All he needed to say 'Yes' but he messed it up. The Lord, however, looked beyond his short sight and mentality and gave him the healing he truly needed. I ask you the same question today, "Do you really want to heal?" The reason for this is, if you are not ready to heal, you can glean all you can from this book and it will still make no sense if you do not really make up your mind to truly heal.

The principal period of healing physically is irritation, you know the body's reaction to injury. You know, when you sustain an injury, you react in the form of inflammation. After the injury has been perpetrated, homeostasis starts, blah blah blah.

You see, healing in our body takes a while, so does emotional or soul healing. You have to be patient with yourself and allow complete wholeness. Many people stop at the first stage, inflammation, where the soul reacts to the pain it feels in the same way that the body does.

You cannot walk with a broken leg; the same applies to emotional healing. It is a serious fact that emotional pain can prevent you from functioning at your utmost best, hold you back, and eclipse your potential to live a fulfilling life.

There are times when people do not even know that they need to be healed from negative circumstances that they've been through; they just feel they can forget about it like it never happened.

This form of denial hurts even more. Do you know why it is because the wound actually never heals? It is like some dirt covered up with sand, like a metal that is buried in the ground.

A few years later, it will still be there when it is dug up. It may be rusted but it will certainly still be there. So, healing is possible when we first realize that there is a wound and do not act like it never happened. We will talk extensively about this as we go on.

I learned this the hard way, first it was the trauma of rape, molestation, heartbreaks, failed relationships, and businesses.

I mean, I could just let it slide like it never happened; it wasn't treated and as much as these events happened at different times and stages of my life, they grew with me, unchecked, waiting to be expressed at a certain time of my life. Pain is to be felt, not denied.

At the point when the agony becomes intolerable, some people will attempt to get away from it and seek help outside of themselves. They can create practices that can get addictive. Lamentably, there are numerous practices and addictions that can be created to adapt to a difficult reality.

To give some examples: liquor abuse, excessive alcohol consumption, utilization of medications, dietary issues, idealism, sex fixation, the love habit, and so on. These however provide momentary satisfaction which fades away with time and the pain comes back in.

Passionate or soul wounds can likewise lead you to make personal systems like – overthinking, looking for security and conviction, attempting to control your outer conditions, hanging on to dreams, self-fancy, overcommitting, forfeiting yourself and so forth to adapt to what causes you pain inside.

Those addictions and practices could be attempts to escape from pain; but they don't mend what is causing the pain. For me, it was withdrawal, then anger, bitterness, big one – chronic onychophagia!

It can also happen that you've felt the pain for such a long time that you don't know about it, just like Kim in our opening story.

The initial step of accepting the possibility of healing is to get mindful of your pain or the cause of the emotional trauma; the pain has to come up, so it can come out. Presently, you may ask me: Pat, how might I get mindful of the pain that I have already gotten used to?

Well, you don't have to get used to emotional pain, you shouldn't! Your background and some occasions come up to the surface so you can defy it and mend it.

That is the reason a portion of your encounters and experiences leave you sorrowful, in pain, and with a sensation of being crushed.

Enthusiastic or emotional healing is essential for reclaiming your power and living your life to the fullest. You may be good at hiding your pain and trying to force happiness but it is only pseudo-healing – what I call surface healing. When an opportunity presents itself and life eventually pokes the pain, it hurts and bleeds like a fresh wound.

The Burden

Ama was a new girl in our choir; she was really beautiful and although she rarely smiled, she had a beautiful smile whenever she managed to. We got close and I discovered that beneath that smiling woman was a lady who had a burden she had been carrying for a long time.

She narrated how she was defrauded of all she had saved up for her new business by a friend she really trusted. Now, she had to deal with the pain of working with this person in the same office a few years later.

Most times, we stop the healing process by thinking that what has happened is beyond forgiveness. We hold on to it so tightly that we don't want to let go. Actually, the burden of unforgiveness or not letting go is heavier than and more dangerous than the pain of the ugly experience.

At this point you may want to ask me again, "Pat, is it possible to heal?" Well, my answer is yes. What kind of emotional pain or hurt are you currently going through? What is the cause? Is it your fault?

If you harbor regret, blame, harshness, question, outrage, unforgiveness and such purposeful feelings, you've really made room for the enemy to control you. You need to crush this change with the reality of God's Word and permit the Holy Spirit to heal you.

Face It

One of the things that stop people from healing is shying away from the emotional pain or denying the reality of it; this even hurts more. I mentioned it earlier that you don't have to force yourself to act like nothing happened by trying to forget; it makes your wound heal in a very shallow manner.

What this means is that it can be poked and made fresh at any time by any circumstance. You have to allow yourself to feel what you feel and not deny it; this is because denial can torment you.

Feeling hurtful sentiments and refusing to face them, as anybody may expect, can be troublesome. The explanation you may want to give is that it is not necessary; but if you discard it, it might just grow into an anthill.

Taking everything into account, we dismiss our sentiments or pardon them. We endeavor to numb the anguish with a glass of wine or three. We withdraw ourselves (like I did). We cut or burn through ourselves, or take an interest in various kinds of self-hurt.

Basically, we go to whatever will help us discard our notions and help us feel better. Individually, we do everything we can to reduce and avoid torture, whether eager or physical. Shopping, food, and alcohol aren't isolated issues with some constraints, but when any of them becomes your primary adjusting method, it can provoke more pressing factors than lightning; this is an even riskier way to deal with pain because it becomes more complicated.

You may decide to buy something new to occupy yourself. would eat like food was my enemy and I was just gulping down every lump and spoon;

but, I put on unnecessary weight, felt ugly, and to make matters worse, fell into depression because I was looking terrible!I would eat as if food were my enemy, gulping down every lump and spoon; however, I gained unnecessary weight, felt ugly, and, to make matters worse, I fell into depression because I looked terrible! I felt pity for myself but there was nothing that could be done about it, at the time.

Have you been fighting back the tears? Don't. We are meant to believe certain things which are warped, like I said in the preface.

Crying is not a sign of weakness. Have you noticed that most times when people cry for a long time, they might just have a slight headache which induces them to sleep and they wake up feeling better?

Crying has health advantages like conveying harms from your body and quieting pressure; whereas, absorbing such sentiments can just poison your body and mind.

In actuality, this is legitimate. When we cover or square our feelings, our bodies use genuine frameworks like fixing muscles, evolving breathing, and so on, and these practices, over time, can cause genuine signs like absorption, consistent desolation, and immune-related issues. If you feel that it's difficult to cry, try watching a film that has similar subjects to the pain you're dealing with.

Facing your emotions basically suggests allowing them, battling the impulse to discard the anguish and not condemning yourself for having these sentiments. This might sound awkward however, it's a capacity you can get and practice. Give yourself the space to cry and let the tears flow if you need to. Be careful also, not to make it excessive or turn yourself into a crybaby.

ACTION POINTS

1. What emotional hurt are you currently dealing with?

2. Do you think you can heal?

3. Write down the top five things that bother you the most.

CHAPTER 2:

WHEN A LOVED ONE PASSES ON

Remember that all agony is transitory.

Growing up in a family where we were really bonded was amazing; we are four girls and a boy, who came last. Our dad treated us like queens, we meant everything to him. He was doing quite well by putting himself out there for us.

After I left college, I made up my mind that I was going to make my dad proud and take really good care of him like he took care of us. Unfortunately, he returned from foreign missions and went down with a partial stroke.

He struggled with his life for two and half years, before he eventually passed on to glory on December 1st, 2020. It was an almost unbearable paradigm shift for me.

We do not plan to lose people who are dear to us, as a matter of fact, we do not think of losing them to the cold hands of death, but it happens! There are times we have aged parents or loved ones and it looks like we are prepared for their death but we aren't.

Actually, no one prepares enough for death and the most painful part is that the family and friends of the deceased always have to deal with the pain of losing a loved one.

No matter how prepared we think we are, we are never prepared enough to lose a loved one.

At the point when a friend or family member passes, it can feel like somebody cut a blade through your heart, it truly hurts deeply.

We need to change ourselves to an existence without this individual, and the more they've been with us, the additional time it will take to mend.

When a friend or family member dies, we have memories to comfort us, yet the image of them so dynamic and alive in our minds can also hurt when we dwell on these memories excessively. Anyway, how would we appropriately heal from losing a friend or family member?

Accept It and Release the Emotion

Shyne was just seven when her mother passed on. She was left with her father, who had to make the decision to be strong for himself and his daughter.

They lived on for several years and decided to never talk about it. Be it as it may, there is no way we can just let the death of a loved one pass and pretend like it never happened.

Somehow, the topic of losing a mother would come up either in school or around the neighborhood and this would further break Shyne and her father even more devastated.

One day, Shyne's father decided to consult a therapist because he became worried about Shyne's recent attitude in dealing with the death of her mother; according to him, Shyne never cried and that worried him a lot.

After a series of sessions and examinations, it was discovered that Shyne had decided to bottle up the sad emotions she felt about losing her mother. She acted like everything was okay, whereas it was damaging her mental health!

We have individually lost a friend or family member throughout everyday life, and keeping in mind that time will in general mend wounds, it doesn't help when our feelings are so crude, and the misfortune simply doesn't appear to be genuine.

Regardless of whether you don't want to talk, discover approaches to communicate your feelings and contemplations.

When I got the news of my father's death, it was a beautiful Tuesday morning and I led the corporate prayers that morning, before we opened to customers at 8 a. m. At about 11 that same morning, I got a call from my mom and I had to pick because she kept calling.

When she broke the news, I did not believe it; I just felt that for some reason, he would come back to life and so there was no need telling everyone that my dad had just passed.

For the first week, I was silent; a lot of people who heard the news about his demise called and were not happy I didn't tell them but I knew what I was dealing with. In fact, I acted all normal back in the office as I had only two days off, for the emergency.

Everyone said 'Pat, you are strong, you are handling this well', but deep within, I was burning – with fear, anger, pain and sorrow.

I couldn't talk about it because I was hoping that maybe he would come back so there was no need to spread bad news. Let me use this opportunity again to apologize to you; if you are reading this right now and still feel bad that I did not officially tell you about my father's demise, I am sorry. Now you know why I didn't say – I was too hurt and broken to speak.

Exactly 21 days later, we gave my Dad a priestly befitting burial and that was when it dawned on me that my father had really passed and was not coming back. The emotional struggle heightened. I began writing some things as I could better express myself through letters but I had to burn them, eventually.

<u>The Pain is not Forever</u>

Remember that all agony is transitory. It might appear to be horrendous, and you probably won't have any desire to get up on certain days, however this also will pass. You will discover trust, light, love, and bliss once more. To know satisfaction, we should know bitterness, in any case. Thus, with the end goal for you to find that sparkle once more, you should manage the dimness.

Regardless of the fact that you lost someone special, you should not let that stop you from experiencing everything you can right now in this life. You have different loved ones who love you sincerely and need your consideration.

Obviously, we would prefer not to limit the torment you feel from losing a friend or family member, yet while you manage the misery, make sure to show love to the individuals in your day to day existence. All things considered, we never know how long we have with somebody, so we need to make the most of it consistently.

On that note, make sure to keep a receptive outlook after a friend or family member bites the dust. Individuals who had amazing experiences with the loved one who passed on felt more ready to adapt to the distress.

This may have happened on the grounds that they felt consoled by the experience, as it upheld their otherworldly convictions.

Allow yourself to feel the pain instead of bottling up. Make sure to deal with yourself, rely on your emotionally supportive network, and take as much time as you need to recuperate.

Your loved one would've needed that for you. I am sharing this because it was another factor that prolonged my days of feeling hurt and stopping myself – I shut down and shut everyone out.

At the time, I was building a business and had two staff. Do you know I laid them off for no reason? Yes I did, because I was hurting. Don't do that to yourself please, the pain will not be forever.

Grow Through it

There are in a lifetime, simply countless days, moments, minutes, seconds, simple glances, smiles and even silences that all add up to become our catalog of memories of our relationship with loved ones.

Yes, indeed I am very, very fortunate and proud to say that my relationship with my dad was always a happy one. He was consistent, fair but firm, a great mentor, and teacher, very practical but also educated and loud about his successes.

A generous, kind-hearted man who always helped and encouraged others to seize every opportunity and experience everything life has to offer to the fullest. What did I learn and how did I deal with it?

We are so profoundly tied to our fathers in so many ways it should not really be a surprise that for many losing your dad can be amongst the hardest of life events. But it was a surprise to me because I wasn't ready, my dad just died suddenly, unexpectedly and unannounced and it hit me very hard.

Upon reflection, I can now share my thoughts about how I have learned to cope with this profound loss. I started this book in 2020, it took two years to make up my mind to publish it.

Initially I didn't cope very well at all with my loss but given a little time, it's now been 2 years (at the time of writing this), I can see how one can benefit from coming to terms with loss from a healthy, positive perspective whenever possible.

I continue recounting the days, the minutes and the moments in my mind each day, counting and recalling every glance, every smile, and each memorable moment – a massive catalog of memories now gathered and more easily recalled and fondly remembered.

Get Past the Anger

There are several occasions when someone passes and the friends and family of the deceased become really angry at the things that the deceased did or didn't do. It happened to us!

We had just ended the funeral service for my dad after he was put in the ground; and we were just saying goodbye to the last set of sympathizers when a group of people came in to narrate some things that had transpired between them and my late father and of course, we could hear only their own side of the story which appeared to be true.

Then we had to deal with the rage of discovering things we should have known about but didn't. At this point, we cleaned the tears in our eyes and everyone began boiling in anger. Most of us carried on the anger but of course, we had to deal with it.

I regularly hear outrage, resentment and rage in the voices and in the expressions of individuals I meet that are lamenting; I see it in their non-verbal communication. It is common; I personally experienced it too.

Outrage or anger is one of the primary emotions experienced when a loved one dies. Anyway there are no responses to these inquiries, so why, in a period of tremendous pressure, do we squander imperatively required energy?

We have significantly more critical requests on our time and energy when we lose a loved one. How do you deal with anger that comes from grief? I knew you'd ask that; read on.

Anger is normal but very destructive when not properly managed and you have to deal with it in the best possible way that suits you. Stop being angry at your deceased parent, for example, who was unable to provide some of the things you required, causing you to experience additional stress.

Quit getting angry over your deceased spouse. Stop being angry at your deceased parent, for example, who was unable to provide some of the things you required, causing you to experience additional stress and has left you with the responsibility of raising kids alone. Deal with it and stop hurting, turn that energy into a positive one.

Another way to move beyond anger in sorrow is to join a care group of people in similar situations to yourself. The incredible advantage of this gathering is beyond alleviation.

When tuning in to their emotions, their accounts and the manner in which they dealt with comparable circumstances will make you feel in good company. It will also help you understand that what you are going through is typical.

You also acknowledge others who have gone through far more regrettable and painful experiences than you. Like I said, I learned this lesson very late and the hard way, I thought I could handle it myself and shut everyone out. However, that wasn't a helpful approach.

Prepare for the New Normal

The death of a loved one comes with its demands, especially after funeral proceedings (For people in some parts of Africa, can be quite demanding and draining) have been completed.

You have lived all or a part of your life with this person; now you have to get used to not having them around or seeing anymore.

v You can decide to put away images and objects that remind you of them, for a while.

v Replace these objects with other beautiful things like flowers, if it will help you

v Instead of locking up the room where they used to sleep, you can refurbish or re-arrange it, change the paintings if possible.

v Give them a befitting funeral, as much as possible, and as much as you can handle.

Get Actively Involved

Losing a loved one has driven many people to find a deeper spiritual connection and move on to greater things in life. It made them build a personal relationship with the Lord while getting actively involved in the things of God.

Ruth was a young woman who shared such a deep pain with her mother-in-law Naomi. They felt the pain at different levels – Naomi dealt with the pain of losing her two sons in a land where they had sojourned; losing one child was enough pain already, but losing two was a very big deal. She had no mother, father, and her husband had passed on as well.

All she had left was her sons and she was probably praying to have grandchildren from them who would run around her, but here she was, an orphan, widow and childless. It was indeed a great pain!

Ruth on the other hand did not enjoy the bliss of her marriage with Mahlon; it ended when she least expected it. Just like that, she woke up one morning and her husband was dead. She never saw it coming nor did she prepare for it, just as we never prepare enough for death.

Really, no one wishes for their loved ones to die. She met with Naomi and she knew she had to make a big decision – mourn her husband and move on or wallow in it with no idea of what would become of her. Of course, she decided to heal and move on, the rest is history!

Ruth went with Naomi and took charge of her life; they both grieved their losses and made the conscious decision to make the rest of their lives the best of their lives. Ruth's mind was so open, she had so healed that she was mentally and emotionally ready to make new connections.

At this point, I'd like to add that if you lose a loved one and you have the intention of re-marrying, you have to be sure you are emotionally and mentally ready for it, so you don't carry unwanted baggage into your new relationship. You see my friend, you are not going to hurt forever; you will heal but you have to help yourself heal.

Healing doesn't always come from shutting everyone out. Sometimes, all you need is to relocate or take a break from the place that reminds you so much of the one you've lost, so that you can have a clear mind for a while.

In addition to other things, this may involve expecting a portion of the obligations and social jobs once in the past satisfied by your loved one that has passed on.

Moreover, if you fear returning home to a vacant house, you might need to think about including new schedules that give you solace.

Encountering nature and the utilization of music, love, and routinely booked telephone calls to dear companions can be pragmatic and it makes a difference.

While rushing into newly discovered serious or close connections isn't generally a good idea, being open to associations with people who share your qualities and interests is essential.

Quite a number of people feel traitorous or untrustworthy when they discover happiness in public activity or structure new connections. It happens but you will need to open your heart to healing, regardless.

Note at this point that the goal is not that you forget your loved one who had just passed, like they meant nothing to you; it is to arrive at where you can recall and respect without being stopped in your own living. New kinships frequently enable you to advance as an individual with hope and a future, despite the fact that the torment of misfortune occasionally hurts.

The significant thing is to permit yourself to lament and develop. You should seriously consider looking for a healing program offered by a nearby church or setting aside a couple of hours each week to pray, journal, or think about your sadness. Get actively involved in your healing process, you can handle it.

ACTION POINTS

1. How do you personally deal with pain?

2. Why exactly are you angry or hurt?

3. Make a list of the things you will get actively involved in.

CHAPTER 3:

THE WOUNDS OF GROWING UP

Wounds, when allowed to linger for a long time, will lead to depression, which in turn leads to suicide

We all grow in different environments with different experiences and circumstances that make growing up fun and friendly or dreary and lonely.

There are many adults today, who still carry around the wounds of growing up and most times, they do not even know where it came from, they just find themselves exhibiting some traits that are considered abnormal. We will outline some of the sources of these wounds.

While growing up, there are some terrible experiences that children face, and this can greatly influence their lives as adults. During childhood, our opinions are not considered because we are said to be kids and know nothing. Most times, children are abused physically, psychologically, and physiologically. These wounds, if not outgrown or dealt with, will affect that child throughout his/her phases of life.

Research has it that 75% of adults today carry that deep wound of growing up, making them not live their lives to the fullest.

These wounds grow with the child, shaping his or her attitude toward life and others, which is harmful to the child, the adult he or she is becoming, and society at large.

These wounds prevent them from seeing the brighter side of life and embracing it. They end up becoming unforgiving, sad, unfriendly, secluded, and depressed people. They lose trust and faith in people.

Children who we think or know to have these wounds should be treated specially, attention should be drawn to them to help them snap out of it, heal and be free.

These wounds when allowed to linger for a long time, will lead to depression which in turn leads to suicide. As an adult, teenager or child, you need to let go of the wounds of growing up, open up and allow those wounds to heal.

First, you need to acknowledge that there are things that happen that we cannot control, we just try not to allow them to affect what we think and know about ourselves. Also, you need to reconcile your past and your present for an amazing future. Let go, and forgive those you need to even without them knowing.

Although some wounds heal and leave scars behind; that doesn't mean the wound is still there, but for you to acknowledge that you were able to overcome and continue living.

Body-Shaming

A lot of people grow up with warped philosophies about their bodies and how they look. They are told that they don't fit in because they have certain physiques, color and weight. As a result, these people become overly conscious of their bodies and even label themselves as not being attractive or attractive enough!

Body shaming affects the psychological and mental health of its victims and they can carry on this wound for life! Imagine being body-shamed by your own family!

If you have been told of how terrible you look and how you are not beautiful, or handsome and will not amount to anything good, it is time to tear off that sheet. You have stayed there for a long time, begin to see yourself differently.

Change your outfit, have a good haircut, get your hair and make-up done, wear a big smile, and put on your confidence because you are enough, more than enough.

<u>Sibling Rivalry</u>

Many centuries ago, people used to live in large families – immediate and extended alike and to most people, it was fun.

However over the years, evolution, economic conditions, digitalization and policies have greatly influenced our choices of family life. There are smaller families and more things to deal with, and one of them is sibling rivalry.

It is a form of competition that exists among siblings, whether or not they are blood-related. If it is not watched, it can degenerate to violent hatred which will lead to enmity and sadly, most parents even encourage this in ways they do not even know.

Examples are everywhere – in myths, folk tales and even stories told to children by moonlight.

Growing up in a home where there is sibling rivalry can haunt the adult in several ways and it is a wound that ought to be healed so it doesn't transcend to other generations to come.

David Levy introduced the term "sibling rivalry" in 1941. He said that for an older sibling, the aggressive response to the new baby is so typical that it is safe to say it is a common feature of family life.

I think that parents can ameliorate this response by being vigilant to favoritism and by taking appropriate preventative steps. In fact, the ideal time to lay the groundwork for a lifetime of supportive relationships between siblings is during the months prior to the new baby's arrival.

How it Started

It started in the old times, when Cain and Abel brought an offering to the Lord in the book of Genesis. Abel gave a worthy offering which was accepted by the Lord but Cain's offering was rejected as it did not meet God's standards.

This instilled jealousy in Cain, and he eventually killed his brother because he couldn't deal with the great jealousy (rivalry) he felt in his heart against him.

Sibling rivalry begins as a very subtle issue but can really escalate and spread like wildfire if it is not handled properly; it regularly proceeds all through adolescence and can be baffling and unpleasant to both parents and guardians.

Teenagers battle for similar reasons more youthful youngsters battle, however they are better prepared to actually, mentally, and genuinely hurt and be mentally and sincerely hurt by one another.

Physical and passionate changes cause pressures in the teen years, as do changing associations with guardians and companions.

Sibling rivalry can proceed into adulthood, and kin connections can change significantly throughout the long term. Occasions like a parent's disease may unite siblings, while marriage may divide them, especially if the in-law relationship is stressed.

The Role of Parents

Sibling rivalry can be dealt with, with an effort from the siblings, parents, guardians and other family members. Genesis 27: 5 – 17 reads:

Now Rebekah was listening when Isaac spoke to Esau, his son. And Esau went to the field to hunt game and to bring it. So Rebekah spoke to Jacob, her son, saying, "Indeed I heard your father speak to Esau, your brother, saying, 'Bring me game and make savory food for me, that I may eat it and bless you in the presence of the Lord before my death.'

Now therefore, my son, obey my voice according to what I command you. Go now to the flock and bring me from there two choice kids of the goats, and I will make savory food from them for your father, such as he loves.

Then you shall take it to your father that he may eat it, and that he may bless you before his death." And Jacob said to Rebekah his mother, "Look, Esau my brother is a hairy man, and I am a smooth-skinned man. Perhaps my father will feel me, and I shall seem to be a deceiver to him; and I shall bring a curse on myself and not a blessing." But his mother said to him, "Let your curse be on me, my son; only obey my voice, and go, get them for me."

And he went and got them and brought them to his mother, and his mother made savory food, such as his father loved.

Then Rebekah took the choice clothes of her elder son Esau, which were with her in the house, and put them on Jacob, her younger son. And she put the skins of the kids of the goats on his hands and on the smooth part of his neck. Then she gave the savory food and the bread, which she

had prepared, into the hand of her son Jacob.

This is the story of a woman who encouraged sibling rivalry among her sons. She was the biological mother of both of them but the reason she picked one over the other is something to ponder.

As a parent, your children ought to be equal before you, even if you have to prefer one child over the other, it shouldn't be so obvious that it begins to instigate rivalry.

If you are an adult who is dealing with the wound of sibling rivalry, you can decide to heal from it. Here are a few things you can do:

v You have to decide to let it stop hurting or getting to you. There are times you might feel that your parents prefer your siblings over you and they may have even treated you unfairly, but you've got to stop hurting.

v Build an external support system, outside your family. Yes, it is true that there is nothing like family but family doesn't always have to be blood relations, family are the people who you are at home with, there are friends who become family by virtue of loyalty, trust and consistency. If you already have your own family, you can invest in them and do not pass on the rivalry, for any reason.

v Try to reach out to your siblings. Staying away completely will not be the best option. You try to reach out every now and then, perhaps by texting, emailing, or even making a phone call. Remind them that they are family and still mean a lot to you.

v Accept reality and choose to forgive. Carrying on the weight for a long time can even cause you to be stunted in some areas of your life, as well as deny yourself of true happiness. So, one of the ways you can deal with sibling rivalry is to get past the hurt, release it, forgive and let it go.

MOLESTATION

There is worse lasting emotional damage when a child's sexual abuse started before the age of six, and lasted for several years

It is sad to say that most adults who were molested while growing up have not recovered from it. This awful incident happens even to housemaids and close family members. Let me share two true life stories here.

1. Banjul was a very wealthy businessman and had a wife too who was successful in business. A

time came when they had kids and demands increased, this made them seek the services of a maid and they eventually picked someone who was related to them. They employed Meg, a 24-year-old girl, to live with them and help in taking care of the children and running errands around the house.

Banjul's sons were 10 and 8 at the time; Meg took advantage of her position in the house, and instead of doing her job and getting paid, she began by fondling and molesting Banjul's sons' private parts.

She warned them not to tell their parents about it or she would beat them mercilessly. The boys kept their mouths shut out of fear of being beaten, but they continued to live in fear.

This continued for a long period of time until one day, Banjul's younger son cried out to the parents because it was becoming really uncomfortable and he was emotionally disturbed emotionally, Meg was eventually laid off.

Now, imagine the trauma and pain those boys must have gone through, and the scar they will have to carry with them throughout their lifetime!

2. Cindy was always withdrawn in school; this was a source of worry to her teachers and friends but they were set to find out what was really happening to her, as she seemed to come from a balanced home.

Further investigations revealed that Cindy had been molested by her own biological father for several years and was dealing with bitterness, anger and disgust.

As a matter of fact, she was not the only one, her father molested her and her sisters and when they would want to revolt, their father would threaten to withdraw them from school, they had to do it in tears, so they would go to school.

On several occasions they wanted to report to the authorities, but their father was a public figure with so much influence and they didn't have what it took at the time.

It was so painful and what was most painful was the fact that their mom was aware of the ugly situation but could not do anything about it; they feared their Dad so much and he kept on getting away with his hideous monstrous acts.

Cindy eventually got into college and was happy that she would at least get a break from her wicked father. During the holidays, she would refuse to go home; she'd stay back and engage in community service or service in her church of worship.

This continued and in her second year, she stood up against her father's act and it made him disown her; she was cut off and had to do odd jobs to keep up with bills. This situation affected her a lot, especially in relationship with the opposite sex. She had to seek help.

Molestation has a huge emotional, psychological and mental impact on its victim and irrespective of the damage done, you can heal. Yes, the scars may be there for a lifetime but the wounds can heal.

Healing from Molestation

In Luke 4:18, the Bible says, "The Spirit of the Lord is upon Me, because He has anointed Me to preach the gospel to the poor; He has sent Me to heal the brokenhearted, to proclaim liberty to the captives and recovery of sight to the blind, to set at liberty those who are oppressed".

From this scripture, you definitely realize that Jesus came to declare uplifting news to the beset, happiness to the despondent, freedom to the prisoners, and solace to the individuals who are squashed and wounded. As your initial move toward reclamation and delivery and healing, you need to lay hold of this guarantee and make it your own.

Remember it. Shroud it in your heart. Brood over it day and night. It is the Word of God; however, its force will not be completely released in your life until you've profoundly drank from the well of its fact and permitted the Holy Spirit to mesh it into the actual texture of your heart and brain.

In dealing with the wounds of molestation, it is important to understand that you're in good company and you're not alone; the greater part of the world is encircled by men and ladies who are battling with the agony of past molestation. Since you have encountered the harm firsthand, you can sympathize with other people who have been comparatively deceived.

At the point when you've laid hold of the shocking truth that there is no spot or stain that can't be washed away by the love of Christ, you will be in a remarkable situation to impart this nurturing message to a frantic world.

This can be an incredible wellspring of re-establishment and healing in your life, providing you with a sense of direction and individual fate inside the circle of God's sovereign arrangement.

You also need to repeat to yourself again and again that the molestation you suffered as a kid, teenager, or even as an adult was not your fault. It's basic for casualties to blame themselves, regardless of whether deliberately or subliminally; however such blame is bogus.

You were just helpless when your victimizers denied you of something valuable and indispensable, and they are totally liable for your pain.

Your task now is to discover some approach to shake this experience off and leave it. It took Cindy six failed relationships and years of hatred for the opposite sex, to realize she needed to heal from the pain of past molestation by her father.

ACTION POINTS

1. What soul wounds did you experience while growing up?

2. What do you think about molestation?

CHAPTER 4:

BROKEN RELATIONSHIPS

It is unfair to rub off the mess of past experiences on people who did not contribute to it

When people connect, they always look out for something good and sweet to proceed from their connection – it could be business prospects, higher connections, friendship and even marriage.

However, these things do not always turn out as planned and we have to face the pains of a broken relationship. Broken relationships are one of the most common sources of emotional pain.

Most people do not heal properly, so they carry on the wounds and even infect others with negative vibes and garbage.

If you do not heal properly, you will bleed on the people that did not hurt you and this is why we find people these days suffering in relationships, from problems they had no hand in; they are being treated in a certain manner because someone else was treated unfairly. This is indeed not supposed to be so.

The other day, I walked into some ladies at the store discussing, while waiting to pick up their orders. One of them said, "When a man dates a lady, he is supposed to date the entire package she brings on and the total stuff she is made of".

While this is partially true, it does not take the place of taking full responsibility for your mental health, and dealing with personal baggage, before joining with someone else.

It is unfair to rub off the mess of past experiences on people who did not contribute to it. For example, the fact that the last lady you dated treated you in an unpleasant way, doesn't mean you should treat the next lady you date badly.

This is not limited to romantic relationships but cuts across the relationships you have at different levels. A sibling could betray another sibling and they carry on the hurt, the same applies to parental, corporate, vertical and horizontal relationships. Let's take a quick peek at vertical relationships.

Relationship with God

Our vertical relationship in this context places emphasis on our relationship with God who made us. In Him we live, move and have our being, all fatherhood on earth takes its titles from Him and being our source, we cannot find our purpose outside of Him.

When we step out of His will for our lives, we tend to break the relationship we have with Him and this leads to a level of pain and struggle, just like the fish would struggle to death if it is placed outside water – its original habitat, for a long time.

The fall of man began in the Garden of Eden, after he broke his relationship with his Maker; but because the Lord is gracious and kind, He made provision for reinstatement and restoration of that cordial relationship through His Son Jesus Christ and the Holy Spirit, who bears witness with our spirits that we are His.

After the first man fell, he was covered in shame, chased from his place of comfort and stripped of some of his rights. This must have been really painful for him and the woman with him.

So many people are moving about with pains and wounds that can only be healed when they come back to their Maker, who is always willing and ready to receive them.

There is peace in Jesus which the world cannot give. If you are still hurting and not living your life to the fullest, I think it is time for you to give

Him a chance. Let me share a story with you,
from Jonah 1:1-17, 2: 1, 10:

*Now the word of the Lord came to Jonah
the son of Amittai, saying, "Arise, go to
Nineveh, that great city, and cry out
against it; for their wickedness has come
up before Me."*

*But Jonah arose to flee to Tarshish from
the presence of the Lord. He went down
to Joppa, and found a ship going to
Tarshish; so he paid the fare, and went
down into it, to go with them to Tarshish
from the presence of the Lord.*

*But the Lord sent out a great wind on the
sea, and there was a mighty tempest on
the sea, so that the ship was about to be
broken up. Then the mariners were
afraid; and every man cried out to his*

god, and threw the cargo that was in the ship into the sea, to lighten the load.

But Jonah had gone down into the lowest parts of the ship, had lain down, and was fast asleep. So the captain came to him, and said to him, "What do you mean, sleeper? Arise, call on your God; perhaps your God will consider us, so that we may not perish."

And they said to one another, "Come, and let us cast lots that we may know for whose cause this trouble has come upon us." So they cast lots, and the lot fell on Jonah. Then they said to him, "Please tell us! For whose cause is this trouble upon us? What is your occupation? And where do you come from?

What is your country? And of what people are you?" So he said to them, "I am a Hebrew; and I fear the Lord, the God of heaven, who made the sea and the dry land."

Then the men were exceedingly afraid, and said to him, "Why have you done this?" For the men knew that he fled from the presence of the Lord, because he had told them. Then they said to him, "What shall we do to you so that the sea may be calm for us?"—for the sea was growing more tempestuous. And he said to them, "Pick me up and throw me into the sea; then the sea will become calm for you. For I know that this great tempest is because of me"

Nevertheless the men rowed hard to return to land, but they could not, for the sea continued to grow more tempestuous against them. Therefore they cried out to the Lord and said, "We pray, O Lord, please do not let us perish for this man's life, and do not charge us with innocent blood; for You, O Lord, have done as it pleased You"

So they picked up Jonah and threw him into the sea, and the sea ceased from its raging. Then the men feared the Lord exceedingly, and offered a sacrifice to the Lord and took vows.

Now the Lord had prepared a great fish to swallow Jonah. And Jonah was in the belly of the fish for three days and three nights.

Then Jonah prayed to the Lord his God from the fish's belly. So the Lord spoke to

the fish, and it vomited Jonah onto dry land.

The major character in this story is Jonah – a man who God sent on an errand to preach the message to a particular people, to prevent them from being destroyed but he saw it as a big deal and thought he could escape from the Lord. He eventually went into a ship and brought misfortune to the people on board but he was shown mercy.

Some of the pains and setbacks we experience are actually not necessary, if only we can cement our relationship with the Lord.

Notice that when the first man Adam broke this relationship with God, he had to relinquish the benefits he enjoyed; imagine someone who was made to be in charge began to hide when it was time for fellowship. He was so broken and ashamed of himself.

When you break your relationship with God, which is your foremost vertical relationship, you put yourself in a place of vulnerability and deny yourself the power to rule and dominate like you should.

Many people are going on in shame, not proud of who they have become and too ashamed to go back to the Lord for reinstatement, that shouldn't be you. Most of the emotional hurts we have to put up with come from paying less attention to our relationship with God.

Examine yourself today, to see whether you are still in the faith. God never leaves, He never turns His back on us.

Abuse of Access

Vertical relationships are the ones we have with people who have a higher standing or are more highly placed than we are; we look up to these people for some sort of assistance, guide and even mentorship. This is a kind of relationship we must try as much as possible to maintain and not break.

Accord maximum respect to who it is due and do not take access for granted. When you try this, it decreases your chances of further getting close to the person and gaining from them.

Most broken vertical relationships can cause soul wounds because in most cases it has to do with a benefactor and a beneficiary. Once access is abused, the flow stops and this can really have a great impact on one's feelings.

One of my mentors shared a story in one of our midnight meetings; he said that he went for a digital training as a trainer and picked interest in one of the participants who seemed to know a lot about what he was doing and was very passionate about the digital space. The name of this participant was Deji.

During the plenary Q/A session, Deji seemed to have many questions and they were somehow woven around clarity and a sense of direction; this however caught the attention of my mentor and he decided to grant Deji access to him.

Fortunately, they lived in the same town and that made bonding easier. My mentor drew Deji so close that he didn't need any permission to visit; he knew about and was present in most of his meetings.

Sometimes, Deji would pay subsidized training fees and free access to some of my mentor's teachings. This continued until a time came, Deji started crossing boundaries.

Of course he had access to my mentor but began to abuse it by visiting too often, even without invitation and sometimes he would come in the company of two or more persons.

Deji gradually lost respect for my mentor and honor was reduced; as a matter of fact, he became too familiar with him that he felt he didn't need to pay for his courses. He felt so entitled! All of these and more, made my mentor draw away, tightened control and gave Deji restrictions for visiting and having access to him.

Sadly, there are still people like Deji, who tend to abuse access to people because they feel love them so much or because they have a special interest in them.

Well, that will not last for a long time if you abuse the access you have with these people and this leads to broken relationships. Deji fought for a long time to get back the access he had to my mentor but he never got it back; it was really frustrating and almost got him depressed.

Vertical relationships are important and require paying keen attention to respect, honor and boundaries, in order to maintain and make it last long. It is almost the norm to feel entitled, but you have to still do what you need to, regardless.

I made a drastic decision to change my circle and build more meaningful connections in 2019. As a matter of fact, I deliberately began to pay attention to vertical relationships and I changed my own convictions about what was feasible for me.

I understood that if I followed similar advances those influencers had followed, I would have the chance to accomplish and surpass my most significant standards.

As a result of my incredible associations, everyone around me began to see me as somebody with the position to manage them to make their own progress. That made a huge positive effect in my business.

Broken Family Relationships

Connections end or become slack for a wide assortment of reasons. Struggle or conflict is one regular explanation, however now and then it includes different reasons that mean cutting off a friendship with somebody you actually care about, who you have or still live with.

At the point when this happens, you need to figure out how to deal with it, to avoid the emotional and psychological pains that come with broken relationships.

The possibility of a family is one that consistently remains together paying little mind to the circumstance, however that is not really evident practically speaking.

Families will have conflicts, battles and surprisingly become alienated. We are relatives; however we are people, as well. Some of the time, our convictions partition us. Like they say, siblings eventually grow apart; it takes intentional effort and foundational love to stay together.

Different occasions, our characters don't align and can result in a series of contentions. Here and there, our relatives accomplish something we simply don't care for. Different occasions, you may have been pulled away from a relative as a youngster, and now need to reconnect with them since you are more seasoned.

Alienation happens, it is the result of broken relationships and can be painful. There is a common term in Nigeria, known as 'Village People". This term usually refers to members of a person's family or biological tribe which the person may not be on good terms with and may want to be distant from.

A proper investigation into its root reveals hatred, bitterness, envy and strife, from broken relationships. In that case, you find people who are members of the same biological tribe, who are distant. A chronic one is when children of a family grow up to inherit family 'enemies' of their parents. These are manifestations of broken family relationships which result in alienation.

Alienation happens constantly, and for different reasons. Now and then, everything necessary is a conciliatory sentiment to make things right.

Different occasions, it requires more exertion to fix a relationship. In some cases, the relationship may not be repairable, or it might require an excess of exertion to fix.

Family debates can raise a ruckus at different levels, the biggest being offense. This is genuinely basic with activities that one relative thinks about wrong, while different won't apologize or even recognize the bad behavior.

After a significant length of time separated, it tends to be difficult to change the lost association. At that point, there are times where nothing awful occurred, yet you just separated from certain relatives, and now need to revive that former relationship you used to have.

Right when a family isolates, it is hard for everyone included. Sometimes, family partitions or broken family relationships happen after huge stretches of fighting and wretchedness.

At various events they happen surprisingly and it is hard to get why. Family associations change in view of the split and there is oftentimes a huge load of adapting to do. Understand that you can't fix or handle a family detachment. It is in a manner not your issue and you should never be caused to feel like it is.

At times it can help if you improve appreciation of what's happening. It may require some investment for you — and each and every individual in the family — to adapt to the change of the family relationship. Everyone in the family should endeavor to make things work.

There are children raised in families where they have to carry on with hurt and pain because of sad experiences. For example, having families where both parents always fight, or parents who drink a lot and neglect the children to fend for themselves at a very early age of life where they shouldn't, at least.

Broken family relationships that come in the form of divorce is even worse; it plunges the children into despair, sadness and thoughts of suicide from lack of emotional support from both parents. Some turn to drugs, wrong association and negative habits.

From broken family relationships, many have experienced deep-seated anger and bitterness toward members of their family and that anger infects other relationships. When you have significant, unresolved issues in your family, it affects all other relationships.

This is because your relationship with your family is a primary or basic relationship. People with healthier siblings and parental love and care are better friends and lovers.

If you have been raised in a family where there is love or the relationship is broken in some sort, you can heal, you can change the way you feel and become a better person.

First, choose to give love; it may be difficult to give what you haven't really experienced but it is possible. Start by saying it, it may be awkward for a while but it will be really worth it.

You'll also discover how to love and forgive the people who hurt you. Pain and hurt from your broken family relationship can be carried for a lifetime. The result is a multiplication of misery.

It is up to you to lay it down and take hold of forgiveness. I know your parents may have failed in doing what they should have done for you; your sibling, uncle, aunt or a member of your family has hurt so bad that it is affecting other relationships. I urge you to take hold of forgiveness and make things right with your family.

ACTION POINTS

1. What would you say your relationship with God is currently like?

2. Mention your family members that you need to give a second chance.

CHAPTER 5:

DEALING WITH DEPRESSION

If you continue to postpone reckoning with guilt, it will keep harassing you

Depression is a condition in which a person feels very sad, anxious and without hope. Today, we have increasing numbers of suicide by youth because of depression. So many things like heartbreak, failure, disappointment, guilt, low self-esteem cause depression.

Every human is prone to depression, but it becomes an issue when you find it difficult to get over it and move on. How do you know someone who is prone to depression?

· Persistent feeling of sadness and anxiety

· Lack of sleep

· Seclusion

· Loss of appetite, weight, concentration, interests, and hope.

· Change in behavior e.g. excessive crying, restlessness etcetera.

When you are depressed, you cannot just snap out of it yourself, instead, try not to be alone, stay connected to people, keep yourself busy with friends, do things you love like reading books or novels, going for a walk, exercising, shopping and the likes, do not starve, always eat nutritious meals; it is said that eating well is a form a self-respect and you are what you eat.

Also, if you have tried to no avail, then you need to go for therapy. Life throws too many depressing situations our way, but we have to overcome them and continue living. Depression is not a disease, you can come out of it and continue living. You need to understand that life does not end with that stuff you are going through. You are strong and will definitely overcome it.

For several years in my life- my early adolescence, I struggled with the monster. I felt

I was not getting enough love and care (I was too blind to see). I was too concentrated on hurting inside and never felt good enough.

I ran into depression, focusing only on what I did not have and comparing myself with others. I was so shy, but deep within me I knew I was not a shy person.

I would always hide my face, so afraid to tell the world what I had to say. Talented and hardworking, but the deadly monster had covered them up. My popular saying became: "nobody wants me after all". I was so gloomy and locked up in a world I called "my own".

I resorted to being a 'man pleaser'. This happened in order to have a sense of belonging. People began crowding into my life and I became overloaded with unnecessary burdens and cares.

I was scared of saying enough as it was the only way to feel accepted. I so pleased people that when I was alone, I would lament, knowing that I was not living the life of freedom Jesus gave me.

I would wear myself out just to get approval and when it never came, I felt so frustrated. This continued for a long time -withdrawal. I kept no close friends for fear of them finding out I was inadequate.

My life became governed by the opinion of others- in all my decisions. Only God knew I was not living the life He expected of me, though I was His faithful child.

At home, I would vent the frustration on my family -siblings and parents. I would get so bitter to the point of choking up. I felt so helpless.

Inner peace was far from me because the monster was dealing with me.

The whole thing was coupled with the fact that I am melancholic- an absolute perfectionist. I would set unrealistic goals expecting them to be achieved and when it never worked out, I would want to rip the life out of myself.

It was very sad. I would never like anyone around me or even the one reading this book to allow this monster because it is very poisonous. My life was poisoned and my family will always get the feedback as they were the only ones I would vent on.

My patient, caring and understanding mom would try to calm me down, though it was not always successful. My courageous elder sister was there too. I secretly envied her as a courageous lady with high self-esteem.

They never gave up on me. In spite of all, I still felt unloved as I was full of bitterness, overtaken by approval addiction, inferiority complex and an unhealthy drive for perfectionism.

Following the deadly monster I was facing, anger set in, I was depressed and it messed up my relationships. I never got happy and I rarely smiled. I was so withdrawn and never noticed the people around me, let alone caring about them.

Frequent and unnecessary outburst of anger towards myself and others; set in. I knew I had lost myself.

To everyone, I was doing well based on what they saw me do -zealous, hardworking and obedient, but the battle was within me. Only a few noticed the true situation, but I never gave them the chance to help. I was selfish and repulsive.

This continued for a long time until I had a friend who pointed out to me that I was struggling with an inferiority complex! (I never knew all these years). You see! This was the turning point of my life.

I sat down one day and asked myself some very sincere questions. After discovering what the problem was, I set out to tackle and destroy it totally. It took a gradual process, little steps that led to great positive results.

Yes! If you relate with or you are a victim of the story described above or someone around you is hooked up in a world of his/her own, then it is time to act because the monster is lurking around.

If you appear to be excessively shy or putting on a false identity, basing your happiness on the opinion of others without which you get depressed; the monster is around and needs to be dealt with before it poisons your life.

Depression has denied many people of the glorious, happy and fulfilling lives they ought to be living. Sometimes, it becomes so bad that you can't even stand your own presence, it must be dealt with!

Depression is a monster and as pronounced, it 'presses' you with unnecessary burdens and you go deep in a mire of emotional pain. You have to deliberately heal from the emotional pain caused by depression.

Emotional healing will help you transform your emotional trauma into strength. You can start to explore your feelings and deepen your self-awareness with books (like you are doing now) and articles on specific topics.

You can also ask for help and support from a therapist, a psychologist, or/and a coach focused on your issue during your healing process. You can use modalities like art therapy, spiritual healing, counseling, etc.

Find and try the modalities you feel called to try, and that work for you. Never hesitate to ask for help because healing can be overwhelming. Do healing work with the person(s) that create a safe space for you.

Invest in yourself, in your healing because it is the best investment you can do for your life, as well as personal growth.

Ultimately, be very patient and gentle with yourself, you are doing your best. Healing is not easy, but it will always empower and allow you to become stronger and re-launch higher.

Dealing with Guilt

Many times, I have seen people depressed over what they have done – whether it was done intentionally or accidentally, they just carry on this guilt feeling for a long time and it affects every aspect of their lives.

If you are in this category and you're reading this now or you know someone who is dealing with guilt, you have to rise above it and heal; you don't have to stay in perpetual depression because of something that has happened, no matter how weighty it is.

Thank God for your conscience which is your ability to recognize right from wrong and hold yourself back from doing what is wrong.

We are sometimes guilty of wrong-doing but what matters most is taking responsibility for wrong actions, making restitutions and resolutions to not let it happen again; then you move on.

It could even be guilt from sinful habits and actions that may have been repressed but you have to bring it to consciousness and deal with it. If you continue to postpone reckoning with guilt, it will keep harassing you.

Many years ago, a doctor friend of mine told me that most of the people she treats have guilt that has not been resolved and as a result, these patients suffer depression, anxiety and fear. This in the real sense just means having an overly strict conscience – an exaggerated form of guilt.

Guilt produces a feeling of estrangement with God, family and the ones who love you; you begin to feel you do not deserve to be treated right and you continuously live in remorse and regret. It gets in the way of your fellowship with God and steals your peace.

Guilt should be taken very seriously because it has a lot to do with most suicides that are being committed today. You just see or read about someone who takes his life because he feels that what he has done is grievous and cannot be forgiven, he leaves a note that says he doesn't deserve to live.

Who gave that order? It is a big lie from the devil to deprive you of your glorious life in Christ, that is why he is the accuser of the brethren who constantly brings our faults before God, so that we can be denied of our benefits; but thank God for Jesus Christ who has saved us from sin's guilt feeling and has cancelled the legal charges on us.

Now, no one can bring a charge against you because you are now the Lord's. Believe this and rise up from guilt.

Another form of expression of guilt is anger. You see a teenage girl who is hostile towards other people, even her family members; the anger may not necessarily be because the family members have done something wrong but because there is an inner frustration of guilt which manifests itself in anger towards family.

No matter how much you try to hide it, guilt cannot be hidden, it expresses itself in several other ways like, having a defensive attitude (this is most common), ignoring people for no good reason, justifying oneself, blaming other people, self-punishment, unhappiness and acute depression.

The Panacea for Guilt

Instead of being depressed and depriving yourself of the happy life you have been called to live, you can face your guilt and deal with it once and for all. It is time for you to heal from that guilt feeling, Jesus has paid the price for you and you have to believe and receive it.

I once counseled a young man who was given to alcohol, he was just in his early twenties. Few years before, he was doing very well and was among the teenagers I coached years prior. Some years later, I got a call from his parents (I had relocated to another city) that this young man who was doing very well was now an alcohol addict.

I was really touched because he was one of the teenagers I was proud of back then when I was still with them. I scheduled an appointment and made him come over to the town where I live, to spend a week.

In the course of the counseling, he opened up and told me a story of how he had engaged in a street fight with some of his peers back home and he was about to lose a fight and had to do something about it. He was infuriated and in spite of several pleas by his opponent, he disregarded it and injured him mercilessly.

After the fight, the boy he injured spent several days in the hospital and after he was discharged, he could no longer see with his left eye.

Several years after the incident, there was a big burden on his soul and he felt very guilty, each time he saw or heard about the boy.

He had made necessary apologies and both families had reconciled but this guilt feeling stayed on his soul and he thought he could find solace in alcohol; that was how he became an addict.

As he wept terribly that morning, he asked me if God could forgive him for such a terrible deed, that he had asked the Lord for forgiveness several times but he wasn't sure if he had been forgiven.

I could feel his pain; I reminded him of God's grace, which is not measured by how weighty the sin is but by the need of the sinner. He then confessed his sins for the last time and found forgiveness and peace in God. The burden of guilt on his soul was lifted.

Forgiveness is the answer; receive it and forgive yourself. It comes by faith because we really cannot pay for our sins. God's love is greater than man's sins and we cannot continue to live in the past.

Some people just proclaim that they have forgiven themselves but once occasion opens for it, they begin to feel guilty again and that is how the process continues.

Well, how do you know that you have forgiven yourself and have received forgiveness?

v There is a change of character, you become loving and of a pleasant disposition always because you are no longer sad

v There is healing; not the type that comes up like a fresh wound once it is touched, but absolute healing. You develop new thinking and action patterns.

v You no longer feel the burden of past experiences, just like the young man in the story I shared earlier. Accept yourself as someone who has been forgiven; suicide and depression is not the answer, forgiveness is.

Dealing with Anxiety

Anxiety is a friend of depression; they go hand in hand, it is like an alarm clock which awakens us to the daily challenges we have to deal with. The choices and responsibilities we face often tend to make us anxious. We wake up in the morning and it seems like another day to run – a perpetual rat race.

The internet and even social media has not helped matters in this case; all over, are posts of people who wear fine things, live in choice places and go on expensive trips to beautiful cities and most times, when we see these, it seems like we are not making any progress ourselves.

When Jesus said in the book of Matthew that we should take no thought for our lives – what we will eat, drink and where we would live, He didn't mean that we should live life like the things which are basic do not matter; He only meant that we shouldn't dwell on them so much so that it steals our joy and drains our energy.

Anxiety is destructive and apart from causing depression, it can make one hypertensive, which comes with other diseases like paralysis and stroke. You need to heal from anxiety; it is an act that must be deliberately dealt with.

When you are overly anxious, you rob yourself of the ability to cause positive changes at a particular time, you become over sensitive and when it's a headache, you think it is brain cancer! It is a tyrant; do not let it ruin your life.

Most people have become so anxious that they worry about the things that do not even concern them – the road to their houses have potholes and they worry about how that little pothole can cause the death of road users and the damage of their cars.

The neighbor leaves the children to play outside and they worry about how the kids might touch earthworms! They are just given to worry, and when there is nothing to worry about, they worry about the fact that they are not worried about anything, how toxic!

Anxiety tends to be more around because man's needs and expectations are insatiable but if anxiety is not dealt with, it can tie you in knots. How do you deal with anxiety? How do you stop yourself from worrying yourself into being sick?

1. Rest: Many people are worn out from over-activity; the stress that comes from it can cause a person to become anxious. Irrespective of what you do, make enough time to rest and refresh your soul and body.

People who work for long hours without a time break are likely to experience anxiety. True success and achievement is not defined by how busy you are but how productive.

2. Socialize: if you do not put yourself out there, you begin to see a lot of things that you could be missing out on.

If you stay locked up in a place and refuse to put yourself out there, you will always feel like there is something you are missing out on and this will get you anxious. Learn to socialize – put yourself out there, make memories and experience life.

3. Be Grateful: a grateful attitude helps you count your blessings and not your losses. Instead of worrying about the things you do not have and the many problems piled up, isn't it better to put on your praise and be thankful that you can breathe and you have been through other challenges? Gratefulness makes you develop contentment, which is a great gain and a solution to anxiety. Learn to count your blessings, name them one by one.

4. Recreation: what are the things you enjoy doing? You will engage in them often to preoccupy yourself and guard against anxiety. Most people are beaten down by anxieties they cannot even define and when they are asked, they may not be able to trace the reason for their anxiety.

This point is related to the second one of putting yourself out there but in addition, you engage in those things that lift your spirit and get you fired up.

5. Faith: faith helps you reduce anxiety; for it is written; do not be anxious for anything, but in everything, by prayer and supplication through thanksgiving, let your requests be made known unto God.

I encourage you today to cast your cares, worries and anxiety upon the Lord, for He truly cares about you and He is always willing and ready to reach out in love to you; He wants to heal you of every anxiety and lead you on to a life of glory and virtue.

Discipline plays an important role in dealing with anxiety because once your mind is made up to stop worrying, you certainly will.

You are not to deny the reality of the things that get you worried but cast your confidence in God, who is able to make all grace abound towards you.

MONEY PROBLEMS

Monetary issues and difficulties happen to everybody sooner or later, and the pressure and stress can get to you. Notwithstanding, understanding that there is quite often an exit plan can help you not feel so discouraged.

You might have the option to discover the exit plan yourself, or you may require another person's viewpoint to help you discover an answer. However, one size doesn't fit all.

In case you're stressed over cash, you're not alone; a great percentage of individuals and the world's problems at large; revolves around money. A significant number of people, from everywhere in the world – varying backgrounds, are managing monetary pressure and vulnerability at this troublesome time.

Regardless of whether your issues originate from a deficiency of work, unforeseen costs, or a mix of elements, monetary concern is quite possibly the most widely recognized stressors in today's world.

Like any wellspring of overpowering pressure, monetary issues can negatively affect your psychological and actual wellbeing, your connections, and your general personal satisfaction.

Feeling thrashed by cash stresses can unfavorably affect your rest, confidence, and energy levels. It can leave you feeling irate, embarrassed, or unfortunate, fuel pressure and contentions with those nearest to you, worsen torment and emotional episodes; that is where you see people getting upset and uptight because they do not have money.

I was once like that, especially in my early days of understanding how money works. I started making money early from my craft but I didn't know how to manage it. I wasn't necessarily broke but I didn't have enough to fund the things I'd wished to do.

The one that really got me was to invest the first mega profit of my business into a contribution that went south. Everyone in that neighborhood knew I had lost money, so I refused to respond to everyone for a while. As I write this, I'm laughing so hard at how angry I was at the time because of the money I lost.

You may fall back on undesirable ways of dealing with stress, like drinking or betting to attempt to get away from your concerns. In the most noticeably awful conditions, monetary pressure can even incite self-destructive contemplations or activities.

Be that as it may, regardless of how sad your circumstance appears, there is help accessible. By handling your cash issues head on, you can discover a route through the monetary entanglement, facilitate your feelings of anxiety, and recover control of your accounts—and your life.

Frequently, there's a connection between battling with cash and poor mental prosperity. Feeling low can make it intense to oversee or manage cash, that is why you MUST read books on money, wealth and prosperity. What's more, agonizing over it can aggravate you.

Most persons can encounter major setbacks in life and business, which in turn impact their finances and soon enough, they run into financial loss. If this looks like what you have experienced or what you are currently in, it is time for you to heal from the stress of money problems.

Making the journey to monetary well-being requires moving past naira, dollars, pennies and financial plans. Most people battling with cash issues didn't have the foggiest idea of how to forestall or address the basic things they needed most from the ones they needed less.

Monetary prosperity starts with the musings, feelings, perspectives and convictions that drive the relationship we each have with our cash and ourselves.

Every one of these spaces is probably going to have a neglected injury based part needing recuperating from an all the more monetarily injury educated practice.

Dealing with Money Problems

Like I mentioned earlier, prospering financially begins with your perspective and how you handle the money that comes to you. Money comes to those who like and manage it well.

v Have the future in view: do not eat up today, the seed you ought to sow tomorrow. When you get money, what plans do you make with it? How do you spend it?

What do you spend it on? As a business person for example, there is a huge difference between capital and profit, and by the time you neglect this, you'll be close to going bankrupt. When you get money, whether or not you worked for it, spend it with 'tomorrow' in view.

v Live within your means at a particular time. It is written that godliness with contentment is great gain; this does not mean that we relax after achieving something; rather we should aim for more while we stay content with what we have at a particular time.

Most people live to impress, show off, send a signal or prove a point. The conviction that you just need more cash to put towards your objectives can hold you back from managing your monetary issues.

v Get a budget and stick to it, share your goals with family and friends. Depending on them to help you stick to your money goals can be really productive; they will hold you accountable.

v Reduce the amount spent on non-essentials so that you can have money to spend and save for the future and pay off debts. If this requires that you cut time spent eating out, downsizing to a less expensive apartment, and other areas where your money subtly goes into, you have to do it, for the sake of your mental health and financial prosperity.

ACTION POINT

1. What guilt have you been carrying on? Say a word of prayer and let it go

2. Reassess your income, lifestyle and expenditure; make adjustments where necessary.

3. Is there something you did wrong that you are still beating yourself up for?

4. Write down the things you tend to worry about. After that, decide to deal differently. If you need to take actions to reduce the feeling of anxiety, please go ahead and take necessary actions.

CHAPTER 6:

RISING ABOVE

The best way to heal a wound is to treat it, expose it to all the medicine and substances that will heal it.

Wounds are not treated by applying substances around the affected area, but directly into it. When someone has a bruise on the leg, it is the leg that is bandaged, not the hands.

The best way to rise above negative and hurtful circumstances is to heal thoroughly and completely. The best way to heal a wound is to treat it, expose it to all the medicine and substances that will heal it

<u>Vulnerability</u>

Vulnerability is not a path many people will want to thread on, as it takes mental fortitude to have the option to place ourselves in this perilous, conceivably excruciating, place. Healing emotional wounds begin with learning to embrace and nurture your vulnerability.

This puts you in the dangerous position of letting down your defenses, exposing yourself to the risk of assault and injury from being undefended. You know, not everyone will accept that they need help.

When you stifle and cover your emotions, that energy is captured and stored in your body's cells, waiting for the day when you will finally have the security to recognize, express, and deliver.

Growing up as a teenager, I was very active, and highly energetic and wanted to be a part of every activity around the house. One time, we visited our paternal home and it started raining. Against the instructions given by my parents to stay indoors, I went outside to play under the rain as I saw other kids.

I was excited because it was my first time playing outside, under the rain. Unfortunately, I became cold and needed to warm up, and the only available option was the bare local fireplace in the mud house detached kitchen.

I decided to sit by the fire to stay warm and I eventually slept off, and fell into the fire. I opened my eyes to see myself in the hospital with burns all over the left side of my body, it was really painful.

As they poured each substance one after the other, I screamed and cursed the nurse dressing the wound but she of course overlooked it because she knew I was in pain. I had to go for regular checkups for a few months until the wound was completely healed.

The reason I shared this story is so you can glean a very important lesson from it. I have already mentioned earlier that you pour substances directly on the affected area of the wound, not around it.

One of the major reasons people do not heal properly is because they are afraid to expose their wounds for treatment. As such, they stick to self-medication and even when the wound is poked a few weeks after, it bleeds like a fresh wound. If you really want to heal, you expose yourself to the right treatment.

To be healed, you have to be willing to be vulnerable. At this point, you could argue that many people have spoken to people, and their circumstances have been used against them.

As much as that is true, there are also the right people who will bring solutions rather than exploit your vulnerability.

Exposing yourself to the right treatment can be in the form of:

ü Taking mental health classes

ü Talking to someone

ü Going on a personal retreat

ü Forgiveness

ü Giving people a chance to help

Irrespective of the weight you carry, you can detoxify and get healed; that is the first step to healing. Many people carry heavy loads and feel they can't talk about it with anyone, so it haunts them.

When a nurse wants to dress a wound, she first pours spirit on it, then removes germs and ensures that the affected area is free and clean first, before proper medication can be administered.

The same thing applies to you, before you can rise above; you have to ensure you are applying the right substance to the affected area not somewhere else.

The Things We Do Not Plan For

As a kid, I had big dreams. I saw some things that really inspired me on TV and I had a resolved early enough that I was going to make the most out of life. Then, as a teenager, I planned my life and everything was so perfect.

At some point, I said I would get my University degree at 19, get married at 21, have 3 beautiful kids with Prince Charming who would sweep me off my feet and have a successful business.

But along the line, a lot happened and I didn't plan for them. I didn't plan to have a fire accident that disfigured the entire left part of my body and left me struggling with an inferiority complex.

Being resilient, my eyes stayed on the plan I had as a kid, it felt like I was running behind my schedule but I didn't mind, so many other things happened that I couldn't control.

I met Tom and we were so good together, we planned everything and our relationship was beautiful; but I didn't plan that he would walk out on what we shared. I was so heart broken and thought of committing suicide.

Having my dad around was one of the things that meant a lot to me because I wanted to make him proud as he believed so much in me; but he passed and we had to deal with grief. Things happen in life that we don't plan for, and let me add quickly that living life so rigidly can be a huge source of heartbreak.

You may have a lot going on in your life right now, from unmet expectations to family problems, to money issues and all but I want you to know that irrespective of the weight of the circumstance, healing is possible; you don't have to go around bleeding in places no one can see.

There are times people do not even know that they need to be healed from negative circumstances that they've been through, they just feel they can forget about it like it never happened. This form of denial hurts even the more.

Every successful person has had their fair shares of failure and pain; and they had to rise above it to the pinnacle of success. At the point when you have encountered a misfortune, large numbers of people may surrender to the inclination that they'll generally continue to fall flat. Well, you won't.

It is not difficult to convince yourself that you will be disappointed. Try not to let such damaging thoughts or musings creep into your head.

All else being equal, keep reminding yourself that just because you flopped today doesn't mean you'll bomb the next time.

It is additionally significant that you treat your disappointment as a passing stage; that is how you can rise above. At the point when you continue to push ahead, center on the other aspects of life that have results to hope on, and continue to learn.

Seeing the difficulty as a transitory stage instead of something perpetual is indispensable to developing an idealistic disposition throughout everyday life.

Any person who has encountered disappointments will realize that it is very simple to remain stuck in it but no, you have to rise above it. Truth be told, this may go around and around for quite a long time or even months.

There are a thousand and one things that we do not see coming when we make our plans, this can be really frustrating and discouraging. If any of the scenarios look like you or what you've been through, you can rise again, you can rise above it. The grace of God is sufficient and is able to make you stand. You need to accept and take responsibility.

Start with being more flexible with your plans, it will help. Let not your heart be faint, do not give up yet, there is a greater plan – God's plan, which nothing can preside over.

God is working His purpose out; nearer and nearer draws the time that shall surely be. When it is time, you will know! This message is for you; when you read it, you will know and your heart will be encouraged, you can rise above it.

The Scars

These days, people are no longer comfortable with having scars on their bodies; as a matter of fact, there are several products and substances made for cleaning scars and these products sell virally because of the level of purchase from people.

Scars remind us of unpleasant circumstances, things that have happened and did inflict some pain on our bodies. Everyone who has a scar has gone through some sort of pain to heal.

What do we do with emotional scars? How do we prevent them from making us drop a tear each time they come up?

Regularly, our deficiencies and fears begin from express, unmistakable events and can be corrected once we accept and recognize what definitely they are.

I suggest these wellsprings of fear and torture as scars, emotional scars. Scars can be the eventual outcome of different sorts of injuries.

Abuse and molestation are considered as maybe the most broadly perceived originators of scars; however, some people who have never been abused or molested have emotional scars.

Those events you remember in your life that are particularly hard to forget, paying little heed to how a long time in the past it was, are possibly and likely scars.

Dealing with scars – those things that remind us of past painful experiences, require mindfulness and deliberateness. How should you handle your scars?

Scars reflect in our attitude to everyday situations.

Who or what sets you off or promptly makes you frantic? It might be a word, articulation, a look, or a smell. When you still haven't healed from an ugly experience, being introduced to anything that looks like it can trigger sentiments like disturbance or fear.

Again, who or what do you avoid? We can end up being incredibly inventive when we unconsciously don't want to stand up to fear.

In dealing with the emotional scars, she had to learn to count her blessings. The same thing I say to you today: look at what you have now rather than what you have lost, and be grateful for it.

It will help you heal, and see your scar as a point of strength instead of a place of gloom. I shared with you earlier, how I had an unexpected fire accident that disfigured the entire left part of my body; some of the scars washed away as I grew but some stayed.

I look at them today and do not have to think of the pain and setbacks I experienced at the time; I draw strength when I see them and it reminds me of God's faithfulness in saving me; it could have been worse, maybe it could have been a deformity, but I have none. I tell myself, "If I could get through at the time, I can get through anything". Heal King, heal Queen.

Change

Usually, we will conceivably begin key ground-breaking changes when they become absolutely fundamental. Recovery and healing, according to various perspectives, require an absolute update of one's way of life, which can be scary, initially.

It requires leaving our typical scope of commonality, where we have a feeling that all is well with the world and understand what's coming up.

To get change rolling, you need to at first set your mind to it. This implies developing an objective mental image of your chosen action, which will assist you in rising above life's odds.

Remember, fundamental, ground-breaking change is required to be enduring change, not just change on the surface, which does not have lasting impact.

Pain changes people, scars modify character. This has to do with true change – the one that is lasting comes from within.

You know that kind of change you notice when you see someone you used to know a few years earlier and it's obvious they are not the same in every way; it is not a mere physical experience.

You may adorn yourself physically with choice and expensive apparel and look different, but if the inward man is not refined, things will not really be set right. You may need to turn inward and set things right; that is when true change happens.

To rise above means to embrace change in every positive way – change in your perception, belief system, sets of values, confessions, and lifestyle.

ACTION POINT

1. Talking session: You will need to stand in front of a mirror and have a mirror session. Just have a brief and honest conversation with yourself and make a journal of how you feel at the end of the session.

It is an opportunity to have a meeting with yourself; it is true that you are hurting but have that conversation, let it all out and decide to rise above all that has happened.

CHAPTER 7:

YOU ARE MADE WHOLE

Wholeness is beyond feeling, it is a state of life, a realm you should operate in

Indeed, it's been an amazing journey through the first six chapters and I'm glad you are reading this chapter now because it encapsulates all we have been discussing from chapter one. Healing isn't healing if there is no wholeness.

What this means is that to say that a person is healed, there must be wholeness. If you stop at the point of healing, wounds might be poked and they bleed again but wholeness depicts that there is complete healing of both the pain and other things that would bring about future pain.

Wholeness

If I repeat the question – would you like to be made whole? I'm sure you would say yes. Essentially, to be made whole means to be transformed into a whole person who is not hurting; that is, to end up being truly well, and significantly well.

The more whole we become truly and significantly, the better we will undoubtedly be truly.

For instance, a person whose life is stacked with fault and guilt because of sin, or is nursing hatred and declining to pardon someone who has hurt the individual being referred to is very likely to be sick really or conceivably mentally.

Ulcer, for example, is caused less by what is being eaten anyway and more by the thing eating up inside. In the same way, when you harbor supercharged negative sentiments, you are likely not to enjoy wholeness.

Wholeness isn't connected to having the ideal life, and it isn't just for the people who have never been broken. It isn't something you lose and never re-establish.

It is about never losing our capacity for bliss, even through the brokenness. In life, we will reliably have different sides – the dull and the light, and several sources of emotional hurt have been examined in previous chapters.

Whenever we experience torture, inconvenience, or a hardship, it's not hard to figure, how should I ever feel happy or whole again? Now and again we feel like we've been unsalvageable, hurt or have lost a piece of ourselves.

Throughout the pages of this book, I have shared my personal stories of emotional hurt and I've come to realize that we release our resistance and become open to more significant knowledge and methods of healing and becoming whole.

Looking back at presumably the most inconvenient events in my everyday life, I've discovered that every last one of those experiences of brokenness were opportunity to rediscover the fulfilment that was reliably there. During those events, I desired more than anything to feel serenity and elation.

The decision to stop hurting drove me to feel unadulterated happiness again, yet it didn't absolutely kill the torture that would for each situation live in my heart, until I rose to wholeness.

I evolved into a more self-aware and sensitive individual, both to myself and to others.

I became more aware of what is truly important in my day-to-day life. I cultivated a more significant relationship with others and pulled in more love.

By regarding and seeing the insightfulness in my difficulty, I had more noticeable appreciation for the enjoyment that showed up. It took me two whole years to put this together, I needed to be sure of complete wholeness before letting others in. I am glad that you are reading this right now and I'm sure you're happy for me too.

We can regard our wholeness by truly celebrating when we feel euphoria, living in the sweet second, and remembering that we were completely made to have it.

Yes, you deserve to be whole. When we are broken, we can regard those feelings of pity by practicing self-compassion and treating ourselves with reverence.

As much as pleasure should not be neglected, neither should wretchedness or ill feeling.

Now and again you need a break to restore, so you may truly sprout into what is immediate – your wholeness. There is no ideal method to follow. In any case, regardless of how you are feeling or what you are watching, make an effort to be mindful and sensitive to yourself.

Being whole is connected to tolerating all of you, and remembering that you are expected to feel sweet, even amidst the tough spots; but wholeness is beyond feeling, it is a state of life, a realm you should operate in.

Encircle yourself with people who cause you to feel much improved and like to champion your spirit, not the ones who only come to sing "death songs" and leave you in gloom.

In addition, specifically, love yourself and understand that all of the turbulent, magnificent sides of your story are what make up the wholeness inside.

To enjoy wholeness, you need to decide to get past each past hurt, pardon anyone and every single person who has ever hurt you, face and resolve each covered or repressed contrary inclination, oversee and resolve any unconfessed sin, and make your life right with God.

Remember, also, there is a gigantic improvement between a need and a wish. To be made well/complete, affirmations must be included. I received a note of affirmations when I began my journey to wholeness.

As I read through the scriptures and exposed myself to other rich contents, I made a full note full of affirmations—the opposite of the negative things that were flying in my head and I had believed to be true.

It worked; it really worked. The feeble never make it. They may want to heal; in any case, they don't need to take it seriously enough to go to the expense of doing whatever it takes to be completely well.

In the first place, we ought to see that we have three perspectives to our being - spirit, soul, and body.

The body is the way we relate to our present condition. We have five senses - we smell, see, taste, hear and make contact. We are also licensed to connect with the genuine world.

We have a soul - a cerebrum, will, sentiments, soul, and mindfulness. We can't see the soul; anyway we each understand that it is fundamental for us.

The soul is our technique for relating to other people. We are considerate of ourselves in relation to others.

At the soul level we can snicker with others, love others, and get love from others, or we can be desirous, perturbed, and brutal toward others.

We pick with our will and mind how we will follow up in the world - and by and large, how we will act toward others. We similarly have a spirit - the internal person.

Healing happens to many people, including, believe it or not, the vast majority, not only in the genuine sensation of enduring a contamination, but also in the significant sensation of benefiting from God's grace.

There were ten lepers who were healed of leprosy, but only one was made whole, by reason of gratitude and thanksgiving. What do you see here?

Wholeness is in a life of gratitude and thankfulness.

However, do even 10% of us understand the relationship between healing and wholeness? Probably not. Most people think little of the fact that wholeness shows up in an unfathomable combination of ways, and disregard the effort to achieve this through authentic appreciation and devotion to God.

Many are healed, few are made whole. That is why you should be mindful of God's excellence and know that you can push toward wholeness and perfection. Not a lot of people know they can be made whole. I need you to be one of the people who believe that wholeness and perfection is possible.

Regardless, wholeness implies a greater commitment to God, a more dependable regard for the possessing Christ. "Every good and perfect gift comes from above, from the Father of lights" (James 1:17). Stop attributing your ability to heal to your own capacity or even luck.

You are highly regarded by an extraordinary Father who understands how to bestow incredible favors on you. Be committed to Him.

So every time you feel an exceptional preview of excellence in your life, pivot to Jesus. Express profound gratitude to Him for the patching, limp fairly closer, and fill in your devotion to Him. Let the things of this world faint fairly more. Besides, hear Him say "you are made whole."

Water the Good Habits

Now that you are enjoying a life of wholeness, you have to keep up the good work. You must maintain a healthy lifestyle to ensure that the wholeness is not tampered with, just as an athlete must continue to train to stay fit and ready for a race. So, tend to your good habits.

Make it a deliberate effort to feed patience, forgiveness, healthy self-esteem and other attributes that will make you stronger. The next time you are tempted to focus on any negative energy, ask yourself, do I really want to stay where I am?

When you water the good habits and virtues, you will see the traits developing in your life and you will be more equipped to make healthy choices.

Research shows that ninety percent of our everyday behavior is based on our habits – what we do when we wake up in the morning, how we spend money, how we relate with people, the things we watch and listen to, and how we treat people.

You cannot keep doing things the same way and expect a different result. Therefore, since you have now entered the phase of wholeness and perfection, keep up with the things that pump you positively, water the good habits.

Cheerfulness

A merry heart is like medicine to the body but gloom dries up the bones. In the previous pages of this chapter, I talked about how the tenth leper walked into a state of wholeness – by gratitude and thankfulness.

Many people have so many beliefs about happiness and its source; some think they need to have certain things, eat certain things and be at certain places or even wear certain things, in order to be happy. However, happiness is a function of your personality and not dependent on external factors.

Maintaining a life of wholeness and perfection has a lot to do with being cheerful; happiness comes from the joy within, which in turn brings about peace of mind. A translation of the Bible renders Philippians 4: 4 as "Be happy all the time".

It means that irrespective of what is happening around you, a smile on your face and joy in your heart can go a long way. Being cheerful makes you keep a positive outlook, in every circumstance.

Wake up each morning with excitement on your face, there shouldn't be any 'wrong side of your bed', like people commonly say.

Tell yourself, it's a new day, I'm winning today, and I'm prospering and making progress today. Learn to say good things to yourself.

With that kind of attitude, minor irritations of everyday life will not leave you stressed or aggravated. Don't allow someone else' disposition ruin your day; don't give it a chance to.

Develop your Inner Restraint

Every day, we are faced with the changes and demands of life and it is an unending cycle; and because your mental health matters a lot to you and you hold your peace dearly, nothing should be worth getting you out of character. Develop yourself to the point that you can choose not to get offended by the actions of others. Let me tell you a short story:

Dickson and Mary had spent their first seven years of marriage in bliss, but in the last three years, they seemed to have lost their spark.

Dickson resorted to secret phone calls and moves that suggested he was having an affair. Mary got to find out about this but decided to keep calm about it and confront her husband when she is ready.

One day, they had a heated fight and Dickson decided to spite his wife Mary, by bringing his mistress Kayla, to their matrimonial home. The intention was to push Mary against the wall so she would do drastic and irrational things, which he would in turn hold on to.

Mary was in the sitting room watching her favorite TV program when they both walked in. After some time, Dickson, who went upstairs to freshen up, came back downstairs to find the two ladies laughing like they were best friends. They were supposed to be fighting, so he thought but they were cuddling up.

Long story short, Dickson and Mary later worked things out and Dickson commended her for being able to develop her inner restraint by not "losing it" like he thought he would.

Now that you are made whole; challenges and circumstances will come together sometimes just to spite you but you have to develop your inner restraint. Here are a few things you can do:

·	Do not speak if you really do not have to. It is better to be silent than to say words that will work against you.

·	Do not change your confession

·	Walk away from the scene for a while, if you need to

·	Talk to someone you can trust

·	Engage in your favorite activity

·	Always have this book, handy

Keep the Spark Alive

Too many people have lost their passion and enthusiasm for life, maybe because of the setbacks they experienced or the negative impacts of emotional hurt; but now that you have been made whole, go back to where you left off and spark up that fire again, it could even be that once you were in love and so passionate and even excited about your partner but now your relationship has become stale.

You do not have to keep living that way; God doesn't want you to keep living that way. Stir yourself up, shake off the dull slot and take charge of your life again.

If you don't learn to be happy where you are, you will not get to where you want to be. Irrespective of what it has been for you, accept every day as a gift, make the most of it and give it your best.

Go back to school, continue your course, go back to work, review your travel plans, go back home to your family, go back to your manuscript and keep writing, go back to church and keep serving, open the door again to everyone you shut out; let some air and light into your life.

Congratulations, you are made whole and you will continue to enjoy wholeness in every facet of your life.

I love you!

Pat Uche

ACTION POINT

1. What good habits are you going to adopt, going forward?

2. How will you handle people who try to deliberately offend you?

3. If you are to plan your next vacation and you have all the money you'd require, what would your vacation be like? Write it down

4. Review all your action points from chapter one to the last chapter.

OTHER TITLES BY AUTHOR

1. Finding Yourself (An Exciting Experience into Self-Understanding)

2. Baronial Persona (Developing Virtues for a Balanced Life)

3. Grow (Tips for personal growth and development)

4. Effective Writing (How to Write and Publish for Profit)